Contents

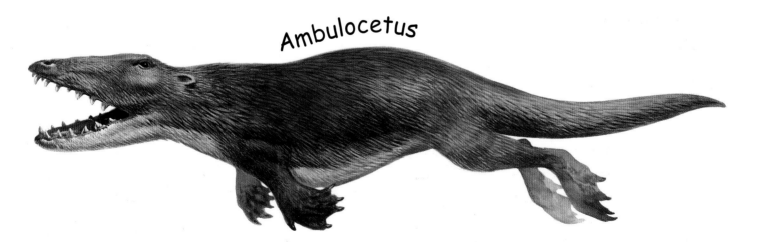

Ambulocetus

What was the biggest land mammal?

Long ago, Earth was ruled by **reptiles**. Dinosaurs walked the land, pterosaurs were masters of the sky, and plesiosaurs swam the seas. About 65 million years ago most reptiles died out. This book is about the new group of **prehistoric** animals that took over. Some were **mammals**, and the biggest land mammal was Indricotherium.

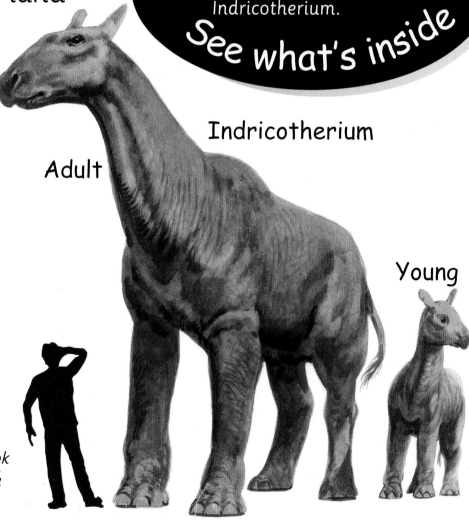

X-Ray Vision

Hold the next page up to the light to see inside an Indricotherium.

See what's inside

Indricotherium

Adult

Young

How big was it?

A fully grown adult Indricotherium was about 5.5 metres tall, 8 metres long, and weighed 30 tonnes. Indricotherium lived in Asia. It became **extinct** 25 million years ago.

No people were alive 25 million years ago. The little figures of people in this book are just to give you an idea of how big the prehistoric animals were.

Indricotherium was a **herbivore**. It ate plants, and could strip leaves from the tops of trees.

Long neck

Large top lip

Three toes on each foot

Its skull was 1.3 metres long.

Hollow bones in its back and neck helped to reduce weight.

Indricotherium is an extinct mammal. Its closest living relative today is the rhinoceros.

Modern rhinoceros

Why were prehistoric rhinos woolly?

Coelodonta was a woolly rhino with a coat of thick fur. It lived in Europe and Asia between 50,000 and 10,000 years ago, during an **ice age**. Its woolly coat kept it warm in the cold climate.

How long were its horns?

Coelodonta had two horns. The front horn was up to 1 metre long; the back horn was shorter. Elasmotherium, the largest of the prehistoric rhinos, had a single horn about 2 metres long.

Did You Know?

Coelodonta was hunted for its meat by early humans known as Neanderthals. Their stone tools of sharp **flint** cut the rhino's body into chunks.

Elasmotherium

Coelodonta

Which was the biggest shark?

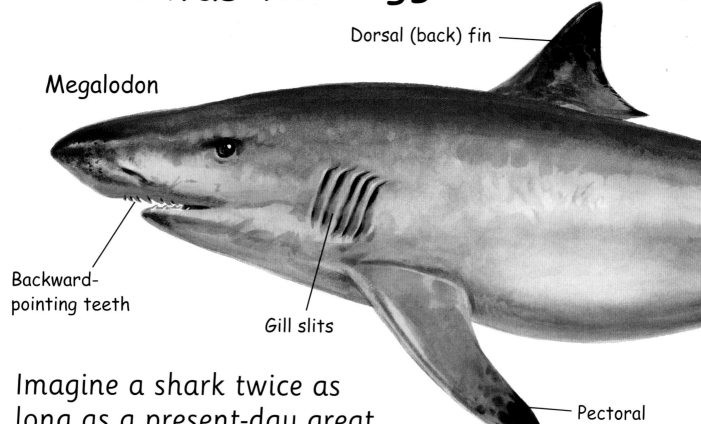

Dorsal (back) fin

Megalodon

Backward-pointing teeth

Gill slits

Pectoral (chest) fin

Imagine a shark twice as long as a present-day great white shark, with a mouth 2 metres wide. This was Megalodon, a super-sized dolphin-eater, 16 metres long. It was the biggest shark ever. Megalodon was the ocean's **top predator**, the supreme hunter of its time. It could attack and eat other animals, but no other animals attacked it. It became extinct about 2 million years ago.

How big were its teeth?

Megalodon had as many as 250 teeth. Some were 21 cm long. When it bit its **prey**, some teeth might snap off – but new ones soon grew in their place.

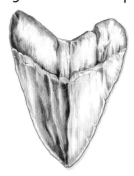

Megalodon tooth

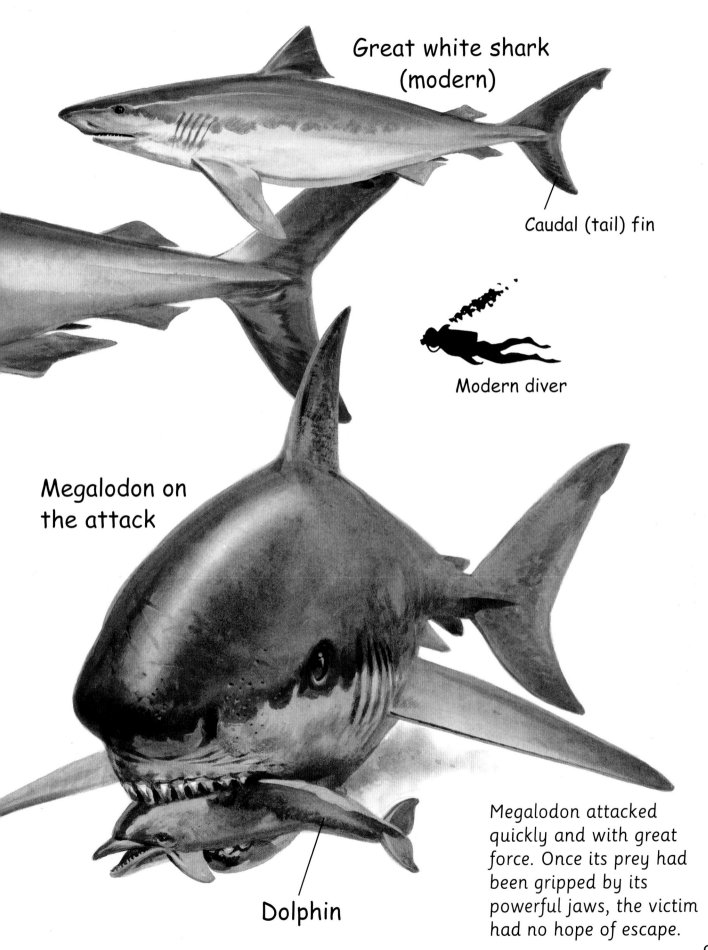

Great white shark
(modern)

Caudal (tail) fin

Modern diver

Megalodon on
the attack

Dolphin

Megalodon attacked
quickly and with great
force. Once its prey had
been gripped by its
powerful jaws, the victim
had no hope of escape.

What were 'terror birds'?

Terror birds were the scariest birds ever. These huge, extinct beasts had tiny wings and could not fly. They were meat-eating hunters that stalked forests and swamps, looking for mammals to ambush and eat.

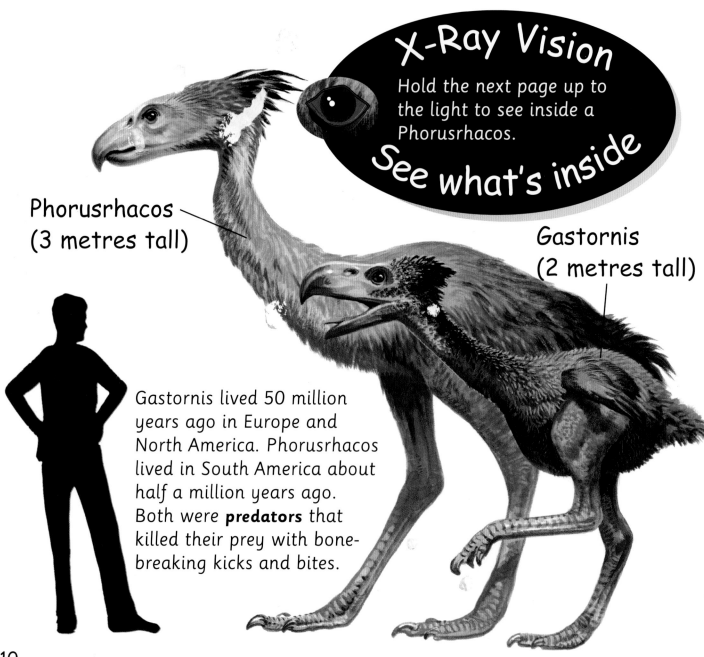

X-Ray Vision

Hold the next page up to the light to see inside a Phorusrhacos.

See what's inside

Phorusrhacos (3 metres tall)

Gastornis (2 metres tall)

Gastornis lived 50 million years ago in Europe and North America. Phorusrhacos lived in South America about half a million years ago. Both were **predators** that killed their prey with bone-breaking kicks and bites.

Phorusrhacos

A Smilodon cub has been taken by a hungry Phorusrhacos. The bird's kicks will be enough to keep the cub's parent away.

Smilodon cub

Smilodon

Powerful legs

Clawed toes

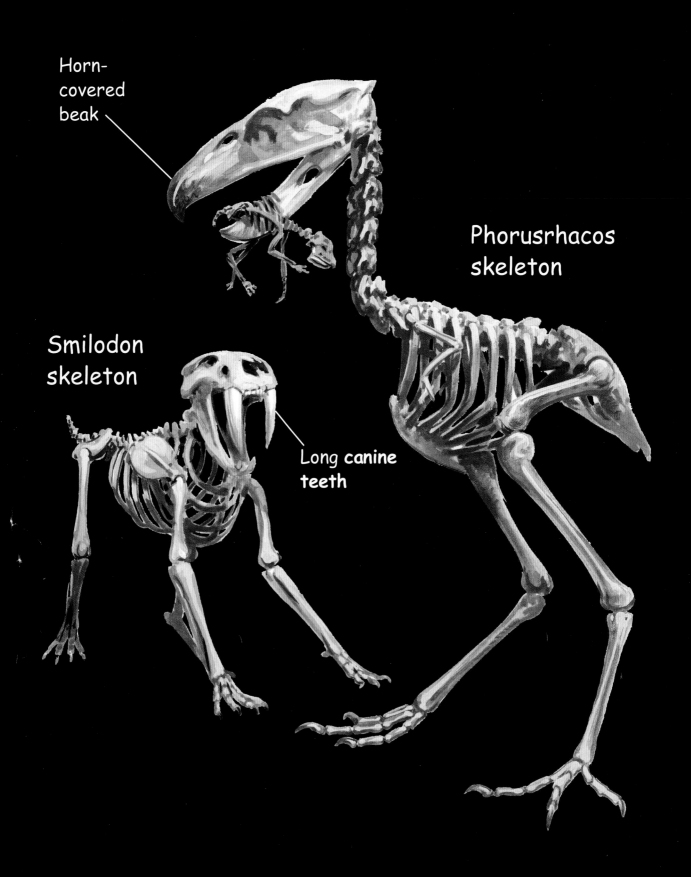

Horn-covered beak

Phorusrhacos skeleton

Smilodon skeleton

Long **canine** teeth

Why did some cats have big teeth?

Smilodon was a **sabre-toothed** big cat. The **canines** (pointed teeth) in its top jaw were up to 20 cm long and curved. Smilodon probably used them like knives to slash at its prey.

Smilodon lived in North and South America. It first appeared about 2 million years ago, and became extinct 10,000 years ago.

What did Smilodon eat?

Smilodon preyed on large mammals such as bison, mammoths, deer and bears. It dragged them to the ground and ripped open their soft, fleshy sides.

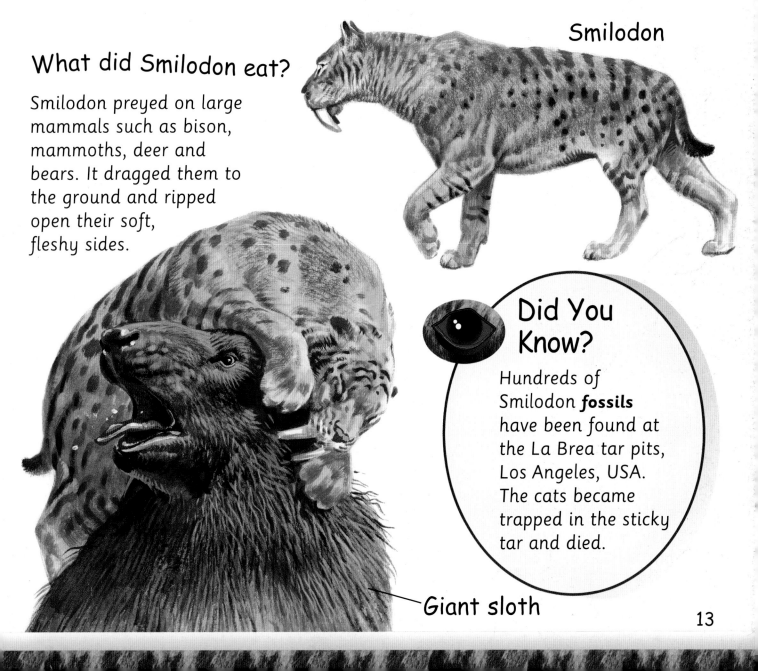

Smilodon

Did You Know?

Hundreds of Smilodon **fossils** have been found at the La Brea tar pits, Los Angeles, USA. The cats became trapped in the sticky tar and died.

Giant sloth

13

Why did mammoths have hairy coats?

Woolly mammoths lived 50,000 years ago, when the Earth's northern regions were in the grip of an ice age. Glaciers covered large parts of Europe and North America, and animals that lived in these areas had adapted to life in the cold. The woolly mammoth's thick fur kept its huge body warm.

High, domed head

Did You Know?

A mammoth's tusks were actually its front (**incisor**) teeth which had become incredibly long. The longest woolly mammoth tusk ever found is 4.1 metres long!

Woolly mammoth

African elephant

How big was a woolly mammoth?

A fully grown woolly mammoth was about the same size as an African elephant – 3 metres tall and 5 tonnes in weight.

Long, curved tusks

Small ears

Sloping back

What mammals lived in the sea?

Pointed teeth

Flipper feet
with long toes

Ambulocetus was one of the first sea mammals. It was an **ancestor** of the whale, but it didn't look anything like the whales we know today. It lived in Asia, and could walk on land and swim in the sea. A meat-eating predator, it lay in wait to ambush passing prey. It became extinct 50 million years ago.

Ambulocetus was the size of a big sea lion.

Ambulocetus was 3 metres long.

Long, thin tail – not a tail **fluke** as on today's whales

Did You Know?

Ambulocetus had ears inside its skull, connected to its jaw. By resting its jaw on the ground, it sensed vibrations from nearby animals

What did it eat?

Ambulocetus lay in wait for passing mammals, such as this primitive horse. It ambushed them and dragged them into the water, where they drowned.

Were there sloths as big as elephants?

Megatherium was a giant ground sloth that lived in South America. It was as big as a modern elephant. Like today's sloths, it lived in forests and was a herbivore; it ate leaves and other vegetation. It became extinct about 8,000 years ago.

Did You Know?

Fossil footprints 1 metre long and 40 cm wide have been found preserved in mud. They show that Megatherium could walk upright on its two hind legs.

Megatherium weighed 3 tonnes.

Why so big?

Megatherium became a monster-sized animal for several reasons. There was plenty of food for it to eat, and it had very few enemies. There was nothing to stop it growing to a huge size.

How did it eat?

Megatherium could reach leaves at the tops of trees by standing up on its hind legs and using its tail for support. It probably hooked branches with the three long claws on its fingers, then stripped the leaves off with its peg-like teeth.

Thick fur

Short, heavy tail

Clawed fingers

What was the biggest carnivore?

The biggest meat-eating land mammal that ever lived was Andrewsarchus. This **carnivore** was not a hunter, but a **scavenger** that ate **carrion**. It may have found food by sniffing for rotting flesh, as hyenas do today. Like them, it probably ate the whole **carcass** — flesh, hair, skin and bones. It died out 35 million years ago.

Did You Know?

Fossil hunters have only discovered the top part of an Andrewsarchus skull. They have used their knowledge of similar animals to work out how the whole creature may have looked.

How big was Andrewsarchus?

A fully grown Andrewsarchus was about 5 metres long and more than 2 metres tall. Its massive head was 1 metre long and its jaws were packed with sharp teeth.

Andrewsarchus

Andrewsarchus lived in present-day Mongolia, in eastern Asia. Its sharp front teeth were adapted for tearing at flesh, and its flatter back teeth could crunch and crush bone.

Long snout

Long tail

Powerful jaws

Feet with hoofed toes

Short legs

Basilosaurus

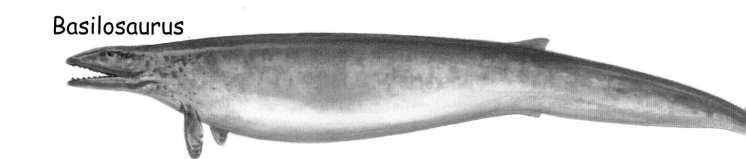

Did sea serpents ever exist?

Tail fluke

Long,
slender body

Basilosaurus is one of the
nearest things to a sea
serpent that has ever existed.
One of the world's first
whales, it had a very long,
snake-like body and a small
head. To swim, it moved its
tail up and down, 'beating' the
water with its tail fluke which
pushed it along. It became
extinct 35 million years ago.

Basilosaurus was 21 metres long.

Durodon

Did You Know?

Basilosaurus breathed air, as whales do today. But, unlike modern whales, it did not have a **blow-hole**. To breathe, it came to the surface and gulped air through its mouth.

Long jaws packed with teeth for biting and slicing

What did Basilosaurus eat?

Basilosaurus was a carnivore. As it swam in the world's oceans it hunted for fish, squid, sharks, turtles and smaller whales. Like modern whales, it could search for food in deep water. It killed its prey quickly with powerful jaws that clamped around the victim. Sharp, pointed teeth in the front of the whale's jaws pierced the victim's body. Then, saw-edged teeth in the back of its mouth cut the prey into pieces, ready to be swallowed.

Who are our ancestors?

About 4 million years ago a new kind of animal appeared. It came from Africa and was a slender creature that walked upright on two legs. It was Australopithecus, a human ancestor. As time passed, Australopithecus **evolved** into other human ancestors, and eventually into modern humans.

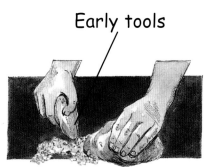

Early tools

Axes, scrapers and other early tools were made from flint.

Australopithecus (Southern Ape). Died out around 3 million years ago.

Homo habilis (Handy Man). Died out around 1.6 million years ago.

Homo erectus (Upright Man). Died out around 0.5 million years ago.

Homo sapiens (Wise Human). Modern humans appeared 200,000 years ago.

How did people survive in the ice ages?

Building a
mammoth-bone hut

Warm clothes made
from skins and furs

Modern humans first moved to Europe about 60,000 years ago. By 20,000 years ago, when much of Europe was covered in glaciers, they had made the region their home. They had to learn how to survive in an ice age.

Our ancestors lived by hunting for mammoths, deer and bison, and gathering berries, roots and other plants. Caves and overhanging rocks gave them shelters to live in, and some groups made huts.

Did You Know?

Sea levels were lower in the ice ages than they are today. A land bridge joined eastern Europe to North America, and people and animals could walk between the continents.

Completed hut

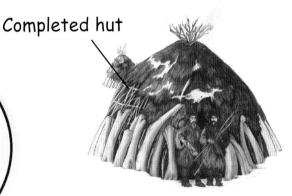

Ice-age **hunter-gatherers** in eastern Europe made huts from woolly mammoth bones and tusks. They were the world's oldest structures.

Why did mammoths die out?

Around 20,000 years ago, mammoths roamed across Europe, Asia and North America. By 10,000 years ago they were more or less extinct. Why? Mammoths died out because as the ice age ended and the climate warmed up, their **habitat** disappeared and they could not survive in a changing world. Hunting by humans also reduced their numbers, until there were none left at all.

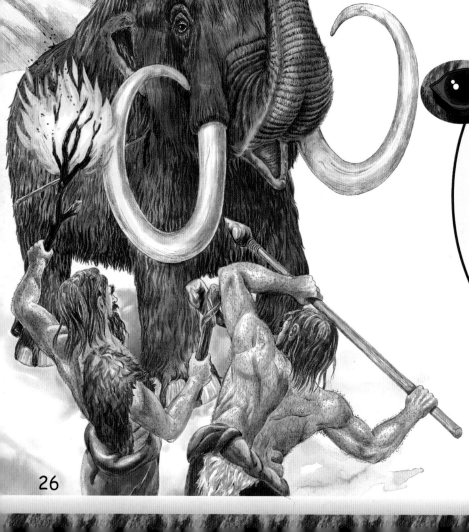

Did You Know?

The very last mammoths died out only 4,000 years ago. They lived on Wrangel Island in the Arctic Ocean, and they were tiny – only about 1 metre tall.

Early humans hunting a mammoth with weapons of wood and stone

How did ice-age hunters trap and kill mammoths?

Mammoths were hunted for their meat, fur and ivory. Hunters may have dug pits for the mammoths to stumble into as they walked along. They may also have forced them over cliffs. The great beasts were killed with wooden spears tipped with points of sharp stone.

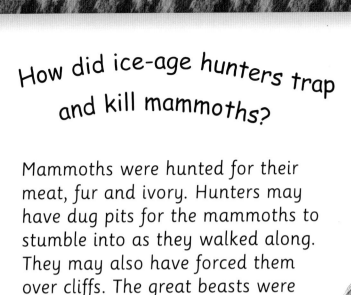

Pit disguised with branches

On the Island of Jersey in the English Channel, the bones of 20 mammoths have been found at the bottom of a ravine. It's thought that the mammoths were chased over a cliff to their deaths. Their skulls were smashed open, possibly so the hunters could get at the animals' tasty brains!

Ice-age hunter-gatherers trapping a mammoth

How do we know about prehistoric animals?

Scientists have found the fossilised bones of prehistoric animals all over the world. Many of these fossils are just odd bones, but sometimes a complete skeleton is found. When this happens, the animal can be reconstructed so we can see what it looked like when it was alive, thousands or millions of years ago.

Fossilised skeleton of a woolly mammoth

Where are fossils found?

Most fossils are found in **sedimentary** rocks, such as limestone and sandstone. Long ago these rocks were just small sediments (specks of loose rock) carried along by water. As time passed they set into solid rock, and preserved the remains of animals trapped within them.

Finding a fossil

| 1. A fossil leg bone is discovered. | 2. The bone is protected with resin. | 3. The surrounding rock is cleared. | 4. The bone is covered in plaster. | 5. The bone is carefully removed. |

  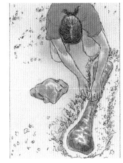  

After a fossil has been dug up, it is taken to a laboratory. The plaster covering is taken off, and the last bits of stone are carefully removed. The bone is then prepared for mounting with the rest of the skeleton.

Fossilised baby mammoth

It's not just bones that get fossilised. Whole bodies of mammoths have been found preserved in the icy ground of Siberia, in northern Russia. Even parts of the fur, skin and insides are still preserved.

Prehistoric animal facts

Eobasileus had six short, blunt horns on its head, and a pair of curved tusks. It was a chunky plant-eater that looked a bit like a bigger version of a rhinoceros. It became extinct 35 million years ago.

Mastodons lived at the same time as mammoths and looked similar to them, but they were not very closely related. Some mastodons had four tusks; some had flat tusks shaped like shovels. Mastodons ate plants growing high up, while mammoths ate ground plants. Mastodons died out about 10,000 years ago.

The ancestors of the mammoth were short and could reach the ground with their mouths. As they became bigger their mouths got further away from the ground, but their trunks allowed them to reach down for food.

The first horses appeared about 50 million years ago. They were tiny animals, such as Hyracotherium which was just 20 cm high and 60 cm long.

Brontotherium herds roamed the open woodlands of North America. These massive herbivores stood 2.5 metres tall, with a long pair of blunt horns on their snouts. Fossil hunters have found hundreds of them, killed when volcanoes erupted and buried them in ash. This species died out 30 million years ago.

The giant elk Megaloceros lived in Europe and Asia until about 8,000 years ago, when it became extinct. Its massive antlers measured almost 4 metres from tip to tip.

About 3.6 million years ago in Tanzania, Africa, three Australopithecus left lines of footprints in soft ground. The footprints became fossilised, and are evidence that our early ancestors had learned to walk upright. Two of the group walked side by side and the third followed along, treading in the prints of the largest individual. Perhaps this was a family group – parents with their child.

Smilodon

Glossary

ancestor An animal or person from which a later animal or person is descended.

blow-hole A nostril or breathing hole on top of a whale's head.

canine teeth Pointed teeth next to the front teeth (incisors).

carcass The body of a dead animal.

carnivore An animal that eats mostly meat.

carrion The decaying flesh of a dead animal.

evolve To change slowly over a very long time.

extinct No longer alive anywhere in the world.

flint A type of stone that can be broken to make tools with sharp edges or points.

fluke The tail of a whale.

fossil The remains or traces of a living thing, preserved in the ground.

habitat The place where an animal naturally lives.

herbivore An animal that eats leaves, grass, twigs, roots and other vegetable matter as its main food source.

hunter-gatherers Humans who travel from place to place, hunting animals and gathering fruits and berries for food.

ice age A time in Earth's history when the climate was cooler than today, and polar ice caps and glaciers covered much larger areas of land.

incisors The biting teeth at the very front of the mouth.

mammal An animal that gives birth to live young and feeds them on mother's milk.

predator An animal that kills and eats other animals.

prehistoric Belonging to a time before the invention of writing.

prey An animal that is hunted by other animals for food.

reptile A cold-blooded animal with a backbone and scaly skin.

sabre-toothed Having long canine teeth curved like a sabre (sword).

scavenger An animal that feeds on decaying meat and food scraps left by predators.

sedimentary rock A type of soft rock made from very fine particles (sediment) which settled at the bottom of rivers, lakes and the sea.

top predator (or **apex predator**) A predator that is not preyed upon by any other animals.

Index

Andrewsarchus